Jesu_,

I Adore You

Prayers for children before
the Blessed Sacrament

10th July 2022

Dear Arthur,
What a happy day this is for you
as well as Jesus! Just think of
His JOY Knowing how much you love
HIM. Lots of love, God Bless you,
Granny + Grandpa.

Translated from the Original French edition
Jesus Je T'Adore by Sabine du Mesnil
Illustrated by bm
copyright © 2019
Published by Mame, Paris,
57, rue Gaston Tessier CS50061
75 166 Paris Cedex 19
www.mameeditions.com

First published 2020 by The Incorporated Catholic Truth Society
42-46 Harleyford Road London SE11 5AY
Tel: 020 7640 0042 Fax: 020 7640 0040
This edition © The Incorporated Catholic Truth Society.
www.ctsbooks.org
CH74
ISBN 978-1-78469-634-4
Printed and bound in Great Britain by Bell and Bain Ltd, Glasgow

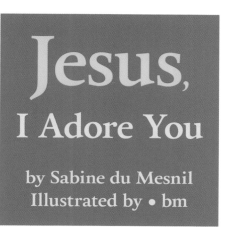

Jesus, I Adore You

by Sabine du Mesnil
Illustrated by • bm

Prayers for children before the Blessed Sacrament

Contents

Part 1
What does Eucharistic Adoration mean? 7

A meeting 8
Lord, where are you? My heart is looking for you! 10
"This is my Body" 12
Come, let us adore him! 14
Going to the source 16
"Happy are the pure of heart, for they shall see God!" 18

Part 2
How can I adore God? 21

Preparing my heart for this appointment with Love 22
"Jesus, you are here!" 24
How beautiful it is to keep silent! 25
Being there 26
Open the door to your heart 28
The time goes by so quickly! 29

Part 3
During Eucharistic Adoration 31

The prayer of the heart 32
Little signs from heaven 34
What a racket! 36
Lord, answer me! 38
God works wonders for me! 40
What if I fall asleep? 42
Little tricks 44

Part 4
Words of adoration 47

In the Bible 48
Our Lady 54
Saint Francis of Assisi 55
Saint Pio of Pietrelcina 56
Saint John-Marie Vianney, The Curé of Ars 57
Blessed Charles de Foucauld 58
Saint Augustine 59
Saint Teresa of Calcutta 60
Pope Benedict XVI 61
Jesus, I adore you! 62

Part 1

What does Eucharistic Adoration mean?

A meeting

Jesus loves you infinitely. Every day he gives you, and all his children, an extraordinary gift: the gift of his presence. He has been here, right here in this world of ours, every day for more than two thousand years. We call him Emmanuel, which means "God with us".

God is all-powerful, and his glory is infinite. He could have chosen to appear in a thunder clap, surrounded by an army of angels. We would be dazzled by his beauty and we'd be scared of him! But instead, God prefers a gentle breeze. He loves us as our Father. He is all powerful in love. And so he has chosen to become very small so that we can come close to him, and see him.

Lord, where are you?
My heart is looking for you!

In the quiet of a church we find a flickering red lamp. That is to show us that Jesus is there, hidden in the tabernacle. The tabernacle is that beautiful small cupboard above the altar. It reminds us of the tent in the desert where God came to meet Moses. The burning lamp tells us that behind the tabernacle door is a still more beautiful presence. Jesus is present in the sacred host. He is there day and night.

The risen Jesus promised us: "I am with you always until the end of the world." After ascending to heaven, Jesus has kept his promise every single day for many hundreds of years. He hasn't wanted to be separated from us for a single moment. What an extraordinary gift of love!

"This is my Body"

At Mass, the priest pronounces the words of Jesus: "This is my Body"; "This is my Blood". And he raises the host and then the chalice. At that moment, the bread and the wine become the Body and Blood of Christ. With your eyes you can only see the bread, but in your heart you believe that He is truly there on the altar. Christ, there before you. He is really present in the bread, with his beating Heart and his divine life! What an immense mystery! Those who are going to receive Holy Communion. They receive Jesus, who is so great, and who becomes so small, in the host.

Mass is over. The consecrated hosts are placed lovingly in the tabernacle. Like a treasure.

When he was a boy, Saint Peter Julian Eymard used to climb on a step ladder and lean his head against the tabernacle. He said, "I can hear him better like that." Jesus really is there, hidden in the tabernacle, and you can come close to him. Like a little child leaning against his or her mother.

"Jesus, Jesus, my God, I adore you."

Come, let us adore him!

Sometimes, very reverently, the priest takes the Blessed Sacrament out of the tabernacle for Exposition of the Blessed Sacrament and Eucharistic Adoration. Jesus in the Sacred Host is exposed in a beautiful monstrance on the altar. Then everyone, grown-ups and children, can come and see him, bow, and adore him.

Jesus is looking forward to your visit. He stays there, in secret, waiting for you. Adoring him is a way of responding to his infinite love by paying him a little visit. Jesus is so happy when you come to visit him, in simplicity and silence.

In the church, God is waiting for you. And you come and offer him your presence and your prayer. It's like throwing yourself into the arms of your heavenly Father. Like blowing him a kiss from your heart.

15

Going to the source

"Eucharistic adoration is being there like a flower before the sun," said Sister Marie-Therese of the Sacred Heart of Jesus. Imagine that flower: the sun's rays make its stalk grow towards the sky, and caress its petals and then the flower opens up to the light.

You too can let God shine on you and give you his light.

And then, like the pollen that flies on the breeze, you can bring God's light to other people.

Eucharistic adoration is also a source of life, like a spring of clear water. On a hot, thirsty summer day, how happy you are to have a drink of cold water! Well, adoration is like a drink of water for your heart, which is thirsty for love.

God is a spring of living, flowing water that never dries up. You can come and find the love that fills you to overflowing, and find love for other people. Always.

"No one who drinks the water that I shall give
will ever be thirsty again:
the water that I shall give will become a spring
of water within, welling up for eternal life."

John 4:14

"Happy are the pure of heart, for they shall see God!"

In adoration God heals you of all your impatience, anger, and jealousy. By adoring you will be completely transformed. You will realise all the wonderful things that Our Lord is doing in your life, and you'll want to tell everyone about them!

You will learn to see Jesus more and more clearly in your Dad, your Mum, your brothers and sisters, your grandparents, and also in the poor, the sick, or the people you find it harder to love.

Adoring means seeing God and letting his presence shine out in the world.

Part 2

How can I adore God?

Preparing my heart for this appointment with Love

In your local church the priest is organising a holy hour of adoration. You have decided to go, like keeping an appointment with Jesus. You don't have to stay for a long time: ten minutes, a quarter of an hour, or a whole hour; however short or long a time you want to spend there. Every visit makes Jesus happy.

When you've got a friend, you want to see them and spend time with them. And you count the days and the hours before you can get together. And when you do, how happy you are to be with them! It's the same with Jesus. Look forward to meeting him in this time of adoration!

What time will you go and see him? How long will you stay? What will you wear? What will you say to him? And what will he tell you?

> "Jesus, I offer you this time
> that I'm going to spend with you.
> Come, Holy Spirit, and prepare
> my heart for this meeting."

"Jesus, you are here!"

Jesus is there in the Sacred Host, and you come before him. In your heart, you can tell him,

"You are here and you love me,
Jesus! Thank you!"

At the same time, you can say hello to Jesus with your body too. Bend down slowly, bowing before Jesus, or go down on one knee, and carefully make the sign of the cross. You can also kneel, like the Magi, who knelt before Baby Jesus. Like that you are acknowledging that God is there, present before you.

How beautiful it is to keep silent!

When you go into the church to begin your Eucharistic adoration, keep silent. Silence is a prayer. In silence, we can hear the gentle breeze of God talking to us.

To help you listen to the silence, you can shut your eyes. Breathe slowly. Try and listen to your heart beating.

When you are calm and quiet, you are ready for your meeting with Jesus. And you can open your eyes again slowly.

"Jesus, here I am before you,
in prayer and in silence.
Nothing matters more to me
than to live in your presence."

Being there

Adoration is very simple: all we have to do is be there, and that makes Jesus happy! If kneeling down is uncomfortable, sit down gently. Find a comfortable position. When you are settled and relaxed, you can receive and accept God's peace.

Don't forget: Jesus is happy that you want to be in his presence. His friend Saint John rested his head on Jesus's shoulder during their Last Supper together. You too can rest tenderly with Jesus.

"The disciple Jesus loved
was reclining next to Jesus."
John 13:23

Now lift your eyes to Jesus, present in the monstrance. Look at him and let him look at you.

Adoration is a face-to-face meeting. Jesus is looking at you. He looks at you happily, because you are his little child whom he loves very much. Let his loving eyes touch your heart, and lift your eyes to him. How happy God is if you look at him!

"Don't be afraid!
Let Christ look at you.
Let him look at you because he loves you."

Open the door to your heart

Now you can talk freely to Jesus. You can tell him your joys, your sorrows, your secrets, your worries, like talking to a friend.

Our Lord loves for you to talk to him. You are precious in his eyes, and he is interested in everything you tell him.

You open your heart to Our Lord, and he opens his to you. In that heart-to-heart talk you can ask Our Lord for things, and receive from him what is good for you, your family, your friends, and the whole world. The Spirit breathes between your heart and his, as a bond of love.

"Wherever your treasure is,
there will your heart be too."
Matthew 6:21

Time goes by so quickly!

You agreed with your parents to come and adore Jesus for a quarter of an hour, or half an hour. The time of adoration has gone by quickly, and you are about to leave, you're keen to get back to your games! At this point, offer Jesus one little minute more: make him a gift of your presence.

Time spent with Jesus is never wasted, and you'll see how happy it makes you!

When you have finished, don't just rush out. Take the time to kneel down again and make the sign of the cross carefully to say goodbye to Jesus.

You can also promise him to come back. Next week? In a month's time? What matters is to be faithful to the appointment you make with Jesus!

Part 3

During Eucharistic Adoration

The prayer of the heart

Sometimes adoration is very simple: you find that it's good to be there with Jesus, and you're happy to spend time with him.

Sometimes it's more complicated: you can't see Jesus, you can't hear him, and you're not too sure what to say to him.

If you find the time going slowly, and if you don't know what to do, here are some ideas to help you.

Don't worry: even if you don't feel anything, Jesus is there, close to you, and he loves you!

If you don't know how to talk to Jesus, let Jesus talk to you, through God's Word. Find a sentence in the Bible that means something to you. Repeat it again and again until you can say it by heart. Then it turns into a sort of tune that plays inside you.

One day, perhaps, it will come into your mind and you'll feel God's presence, his strength, at your side.

"When your words came,
I devoured them;
your word was my delight
and the joy of my heart."
Jeremiah 15:16

Little signs from heaven

Sometimes it's hard to concentrate for the whole time during adoration. Are you starting to look around you? Don't worry. On the altar and all around, you can see things that will help you to turn to God again.

You can admire the monstrance that shows Jesus in the Sacred Host. It is a wonderful jewel that holds the Body of Jesus. Shining rays surround Jesus, our most precious treasure. Jesus in the Sacred Host is like a sun that lights up the whole world and brings warmth to your heart.

On the altar and in other parts of the church, lots of candles are burning. They are a sign of the presence of God, the light of the world. Jesus is the light, the one who guides you through the night, who makes you feel safe when you are afraid, and warms you when you are feeling cold. If you feel confused, ask Jesus to come and shed his light on you straight away!

Can you see the little stand that the monstrance is placed on? It's called a Tabor, which was the name of the mountain in Galilee where Jesus was transfigured, and three of his apostles saw him shining with radiant light. Mount Tabor was the place where they met him, and the little "Tabor" on the altar is the meeting place for you and Jesus today. Are you ready to meet Jesus?

Don't forget: a whole crowd of angels are adoring God with you. They are there, close to you, even though you can't see them.

"I heard the sound of an immense number
of angels gathered round the throne...
there were ten thousand times ten thousand
of them and thousands upon thousands."

Apocalypse 5:11

What a racket!

Sometimes thoughts jostle together inside your head and you don't seem to be thinking about Jesus at all. Because you're thinking about the racing track you're building for your cars, the game of catch you had during this morning's break, the chocolate cake you made, going to stay with your Nan and Grandad, a quarrel with your brother or sister and lots of other things besides!

Don't worry: tell Jesus about all these things right now. He's interested in you and everything you're thinking about! Talk to him about the things that make you happy and the things that make you sad. He will do something for you, you can be sure about that.

Don't be afraid. Jesus loves you the way you are, with your doubts, your defects, your weaknesses, but also your good qualities and your talents. All of it!

"You are precious in my eyes, and I love you,
Do not be afraid, for I am with you."
Isaiah 43:4-5

Lord, answer me!

All around you there are people suffering from illness, loneliness, quarrels. There's always a war going on somewhere. Perhaps you are feeling a bit downhearted because God doesn't answer your prayers.

It's a real mystery. God does not always give us what we ask for in the way we expect. Prayer is not a magic spell! But we have to keep trusting. God wants you to be happy. Through prayer he may give you the strength to put up with bad things that happen. He is close to you, like a friend, like a father.

"Your Father knows what you need
before you ask him."
Matthew 6:8

Sometimes, you don't feel anything at all! You don't even know if God is really there. So why bother going to visit Jesus, you might think. Wrong! Even great saints, like Mother Teresa, went through times of abandonment, the dark night of the soul. They remained faithful, they kept praying, every single day. You might find yourself doubting, but you can be sure that God loves you. So even when it's hard, stay faithful to your Eucharistic adoration: it's worth continuing to travel along the path with God.

"Whoever remains in me,
with me in him,
bears fruit in plenty."
John 15:5

God works wonders for me!

In Jesus's presence, think about your own story. What nice things have happened to you today? Or this week? This year? Since you were born? Take time to remember, with Jesus, all the good things he has done for you and with you. See how much he loves you. Ask him to help you see the little details of your life that you have forgotten. He never forgets you!

Thank him for your family, for all the things he has given you, and even things he hasn't given you yet! Now it's up to you to finish off the list of little things that you can thank God for.

"I shall not forget you.
Look, I have engraved you on
the palms of my hands."
Isaiah 49:15-16

The sun shining in the sky
A hug from Mum
A game with Dad
Nan's cooking
A good mark at school
A walk in the forest
A giggle with my friends
The good priests at the local church
My baby sister's smile
A story from Grandad
A pretty flower from a meadow

What if I fall asleep?

Don't worry! It doesn't matter. When you wake up you realise that Jesus is still there, with his Heart wide open to you. He's watching over you, as he always does. Even when you're asleep he still loves you. It's great!

(But that doesn't mean you should bring a pillow with you to Eucharistic adoration! Like any friend, it makes God happy when you come and talk to him.)

"It is God who provides for his beloved
as they sleep."

Psalm 127:2

Little tricks

Make a little list of the things you would like to tell Jesus - your heart's desires, things that make you sad, people you want to pray for. Then when you go to Eucharistic adoration, you can take the list and read it to Jesus!

Ask Mum or Dad for a nice-looking notebook. At home, or at Mass, make a note of God's words that touch you, or that give you strength. The ones that make you think, "This is Jesus speaking to me today!" Take the notebook with you to adoration to re-read and savour them.

Think of someone in your class who doesn't know Jesus very well, and pray for him or her during Eucharistic adoration. Perhaps it will lead to a wonderful conversation. And, who knows?, that person may come with you to the adoration next time!

Learn a hymn of adoration. You can sing it under your breath, telling Jesus again and again how much you love him.

Make Jesus a promise, and, with his help, at Eucharistic adoration, think about what you could do to keep your promise.

Part 4
Words of adoration

In the Bible

"I hold myself in quiet and silence,
like a little child in its mother's arms."

Psalm 131:2

A very small child, a baby, rests in his mother's arms. He is close to his mother's heart, and she rocks him gently... He can feel how much he is loved!

Just like that, in adoration, close to Jesus's Heart, you can leave your fears behind. You are like a small child in God's arms, and your heart is at rest.

God of infinite tenderness, we praise you!

"I will delight and rejoice in your faithful love!
You have seen my misery, and witnessed
the miseries of my soul."

Psalm 31:8

God loves you infinitely, just as you are. With every single one of your good qualities, every single one of your weaknesses. Don't be afraid to ask him to help you when you feel sad. You will see how happy it makes you to be loved by God exactly as you are!

Then you will feel like dancing for joy! (Even the great King David, in the Bible, started to dance when the Ark of the Covenant entered Jerusalem. He was so happy to know that God was with him all the days of his life.)

"The Lord is my shepherd,
I lack nothing.
In grassy meadows
he lets me lie."

Psalm 23:1-2

A shepherd guides his sheep to what is best for them:
green grass, shade, water. The Lord takes care of you
just like that, so you have no need to fear. He watches
over you and guides you. You can trust him because
he wants you to be happy. You are like his little lamb.

"This is my Body,
given for you."
Luke 22:19

The wafer of bread that is there in front of you is really the Body of Jesus. He offered himself for you on the cross. He died and rose from the dead for you. At each Mass, the bread becomes the Body of Jesus. At Eucharistic adoration, it is really him you are looking at. You are looking at God.

In the times of Jesus – and today too – this commandment was a prayer said by all Jewish people every day. Everyone knew it by heart. The whole family would say it together, from sunrise to sunset, even to the youngest! They said it when travelling, and wrote it on the doors of their houses. It is a good prayer for you to repeat during Eucharistic adoration. It will write itself on your heart, helping you to love God more and more.

"Let the little children come to me;
do not stop them; for it is to such as these
that the kingdom of God belongs."

Mark 10:14

Jesus blesses children, and waits for them with his arms wide open! When he is present, at adoration, he is waiting for you! Don't be afraid, get close to him.

Our Lady

Mary has said yes to God, and she is going to give birth to Jesus, the Son of God. Her heart is overflowing with happiness. She goes running to announce the news to her cousin Elisabeth, and calls out:

"The Almighty has done great things for me. Holy is his name!"

Luke 1:49

Here on earth, Mary carried Jesus in her arms. She fed him, loved him, and contemplated him for thirty three years! So now, at each Mass and each adoration, she is always there. Close to her Son and close to us.

Mary, help me to love Jesus! Make him grow in me! Help me to see all the great things that Jesus does in my life!

Saint Francis of Assisi

Saint Francis lived in Italy, between the twelfth and thirteenth centuries. He had an enormous love for Jesus Christ, and this was especially shown in his adoration of the Blessed Sacrament.

"What wonderful majesty, what amazing kindness!
For the Lord of the universe
to humble himself like this
and hide under the form
of a little bread!
Humble yourselves, make yourselves little,
that you may be raised up by him.
Keep nothing for yourselves,
so that he who has given himself totally to you
may receive you totally."

Saint Francis of Assisi

Jesus makes himself little and humble in order to meet us. He is here in front of us, and we can offer him our hearts.

Jesus, you are truly here in front of me. Help me to stay humble and little in front of you, because you come to meet me. Thank you!

Saint Pio of Pietrelcina

Padre Pio was a Capuchin monk and priest from the south of Italy. Like Saint Francis of Assisi, he received the stigmata, so he suffered like Jesus on the cross...to change men's hearts.

> "Yes, Jesus, I love you and I feel the need to love you even more; but, Jesus, I haven't got any more love left in my heart. You know that I've given it all to you. If you want more love, take my heart and fill it with your love, and then command me to love you. Please, do this, grant my desire. Amen."
>
> Padre Pio

Sometimes it's quite hard to love. You feel completely dry! God, who is total love, can come and fill up the reservoir of love in your heart.

Come, Lord, into my heart!

Saint John-Marie Vianney
The Curé of Ars

Saint John-Marie Vianney is the patron saint of all the priests in the world. He spent hours hearing confessions and praying in front of the Blessed Sacrament. He would point to the tabernacle and say, "He's there, he's there, in the sacrament of his Love."

"I love you, O my God,
and my only desire
is to love you
to the very last moment of my life."
Saint John-Marie Vianney

Close to Jesus in the Blessed Sacrament, you're not afraid of anything. Do you want to stay closely united to him this week? Tell him again and again, "I love you. Stay with me, Lord!"

Blessed Charles de Foucauld

Charles de Foucauld was a soldier at first, and lived his life far from God. But one day he fell in love with the desert...and with Jesus. At the end of his life he spent hours praying to the Blessed Sacrament in a little chapel he built in the middle of the desert. And he meditated on the words Jesus spoke on the cross.

"O God my Father,
I abandon myself to you.
Do whatever you want with me.
Whatever you do with me,
I will thank you.
I give my soul into your hands.
I give it to you, my God,
with all the love of my heart
because you are my Father."
Blessed Charles de Foucauld

Today, every little thing I do, I want to do as well as I can, with love. I entrust myself to you, Lord. Give me, every moment, the grace to do good with love, no matter what happens.

Saint Augustine

Saint Augustine was born in Algeria, and was very intelligent. He looked for God in many different ways, and after a long time he found him in his own heart! Later Saint Augustine became the Bishop of Hippo. He is known as a Doctor of the Church and one of the Fathers of the Church.

"You have made us for yourself,
and our heart is restless
until it rests in you."

Saint Augustine

God, where can I find you? Sometimes it's noise that keeps me from you, and sometimes it's my own doubts. So I will get inside my own heart, in silence. God is there. I come there and find him, the one who has loved me since before I was born: God, who I can't live without!

Saint Teresa of Calcutta

Mother Teresa was a religious of the Missionaries of Charity in India. She looked after people nobody cared about – street children, the homeless, the dying. She saw the face of Jesus in each of them. As Superior of her community she decided to hold one hour's Exposition and Eucharistic adoration every day. Since then more and more women have joined the Sisters of Charity, and they have had more and more love with which to serve and love the poor.

> "Jesus is my God.
> Jesus is my Spouse.
> Jesus is my Life.
> Jesus is my only Love.
> Jesus is my All in All.
> Jesus is my Everything."
>
> Saint Teresa of Calcutta

And I too, kneeling before Jesus in adoration, come to draw from him the strength to smile, serve, love, and console people. Help me, Jesus, to see you in each of my neighbours!

Pope Benedict XVI

Pope Benedict XVI visited Lourdes, France, on 14th September 2008. With thousands of pilgrims he adored Jesus in a Eucharistic procession.

"Lord Jesus, You are here!
And you, my brothers, my sisters, my friends,
You are here, with me, in his presence!
We contemplate him.
We adore him.
We love him.
We seek to grow in love for him."
Pope Benedict XVI

Like the whole Church, we meet Jesus in the Blessed Eucharist. Together, we adore him, and so the love between us grows.

Jesus, teach me, together with my brothers and sisters, to contemplate you and see your face in all those around me. Stay with me all the days of my life.

Jesus, I adore you!

Adoring means "being there", close to Jesus. Like Jesus. Just there, present.

Do you want to become a person who brings love, peace and joy to the world? The world needs it so much!

Come and draw out love, peace and joy from the Heart of Jesus. He is waiting for you! Come and find him, come and adore him!

"I'm coming to you, Jesus."

I am going to the Exposition of the Blessed
Sacrament and Eucharist Adoration

on

....

from

....

to

....

at the church of

....